INLAND

Kay Syrad

INDEPENDENT INNOVATIVE INTERNATIONAL

Published by Cinnamon Press
Meirion House
Tanygrisiau
Blaenau Ffestiniog
Gwynedd, LL41 3SU
www.cinnamonpress.com

ISBN: 978-1-78864-023-7

British Library Cataloguing in Publication Data. A CIP record for this book can be obtained from the British Library.

Designed and typeset in Palatino by Cinnamon Press. Printed in Poland.

Cover design by Adam Craig from Andrzej Jackowski's painting, 'Vigilant Dreamer 2' used with kind permission.

Cinnamon Press is represented in the UK by Inpress Ltd and in Wales by the Welsh Books Council.

Acknowledgements

Versions of some of these poems have appeared in the journals *Artemis Poetry, Envoi, Frogmore Papers,* in the anthology *Her Wings of Glass* (eds) Myra Schneider, Penelope Shuttle & Dilys Wood, Second Light Publications (2014), *The Needlewriters' Anthology* (2015), the Winchester Poetry Competition 2017 anthology *Somewhere to keep the rain* (selected by Sarah Howe); and online at The Poetry School, Slipstream Poets, Spacecraft Voyage Project 8, and visualverse.org. 'Nomenclature' was nominated for the Forward Prize Best Single Poem category. I am thankful for a grant from The Society of Authors' Authors' Foundation, which helped me to complete this collection. Special thanks are due to all the poets in the two regular workshop groups I belong to, in particular to Clare Best for her close reading of the manuscript. I am most grateful to Jan Fortune, Chris Drury, and Andrzej Jackowski for permission to reproduce his painting, *Vigilant Dreamer 2.*

Contents

For Chris Drury

Inland

How individual it is,

each person selecting the right pair of scissors
to cut the fabric, thumb and forefinger precisely
placed to exert pressure, each person standing
or bending close to the other, the fabric whole
at first and afterwards sliding away in ruins.

Over there, always, the drill of stitching and here
the cutting goes on, the standing goes on and on
and the bending, and the garments spoil in tubs
while the body's seamless dream quietly fissures.

Transcript

at first I was struck by the smell
a sense of decay
something static [right palm faces out]
though we know now that things are growing there
it seemed a sad place
I was overwhelmed by the damp
but the next time I went
the light was flowing
lifting the ground and the walls
[arms raised in holding gesture]
so that they merged
life had entered [laughs]
and because the light was moving
there seemed to be any kind of possibility
[hands open, shrugs shoulders]
that first time I had to go down much further
crawl on my hands and knees
the arches seemed lower
and I was surprised when I went there again
and everything was much taller
the flickering light
changed the scale completely
[makes circular movement with hand]
I was no longer aware of being contained
I felt relief   a kind of wonder
I didn't know what to do about this wondrous—
[hands] I can just be in it
and I don't have to stare at it
it's happening over me and on me
it altered time   in a way
it didn't matter that time had gone by
yes the main sensation was wonder
being carried forward
that feeling that anything is achievable
going upward as if the top of my head
was no longer entirely necessary
as if one's own boundaries [rubs sides of torso]
could expand [hands make shape]
the mind could expand into the space [nods]
and that's what happened also in the corridor

like a tide
a feeling of the universal
being carried forward out and back
and maybe that's what wonder is
being transported out of the individual
and that's also the relief *[laughs]*
a kind of finality
I was only concerned with looking *[rubs neck]*
but it seemed to come from here *[touches stomach]*
as if there was something down here
[points to stomach] something tied up
that gets from here to the eyes
without me noticing

Battleship Potemkin

I saw the caught sails edging forward
        not smooth but in sweeps
        sails like tethered mercury
tautness of the dark sails   curve of the sails to the sea wind

I noticed the men's eyes tipped away
        (their cheekbones! their stripped shoulders!)
I became aware of sound   the symphony
        advance of boots on the steps   the mothers
        the great guns rolling up and rolling down
I followed them   *Hearts forward!*   my heart elapsing
        until a single breath shook free the sailors' arms   caps
        and all cried up together
Comrades   Comrades   Comrades!

And still I see those stretched sails   their effort
        and the cargo   birds   piglets   baskets of eggs
        the lifting and passing from man to man
of the geese   wings open   upside down   alive.

This day

It is a quarter to six, already light, I am trembling
and I say 'I wish you didn't—.' 'I don't,' he says.
'But you're always—.' 'I don't—I do not.'

I go downstairs, make a pot of tea, choose mugs,
pour milk. He appears. 'I don't.' Very slowly
he presses tobacco on to a paper, licks, rolls,

goes outside to smoke. 'I don't,' he says, through
the doorway. We are at the threshold—again
and I drive to the station wearing dark glasses.

At the archive, the course leader greets us, one
by one; we listen and speak, raise the kept letters
from their boxes. The air thickens as we dwell,

not finding what we want, wanting what we find.
I hold the breathing paper up to the light—
her writing slants this way and on the other side

that way, just like the thoughts. *'No one can know
another person,'* she writes. *'He said I am —, but
I am not. I am not—and I am striving for patience.'*

Nomenclature

bird's-claw beard-moss
    oblique-mouthed beardless-moss
        swan-necked apple-moss
mamillate plait-moss
    level-pearl
        depressed feathermoss
slender mouse-tail moss
    slender cruet-moss
lance-leaved pottia
    pellucid four-tooth moss
        herzog's pocketmoss
        turgid scorpion-moss
silky forklet-moss
    nervéd leskéa

pseudotaxiphyllum elegance (elegant silk-moss)
    rhytidiadelphus squarrosus (springy turf-moss)
  entosthodon obtusus (blunt cord-moss)

I call your name
    summon your name
        I summon your name in the dreaming air

summon your name from Silesian velvet
    a down bonnet
        arrayed with stars

or call up—mouth(e)—your name
    hold my eye's memory
        of protrusion (nipple, notch, scallop)

ah—our fresh fingertips

Six and a half acres

fifty per cent shaded netting, polytunnels, glasshouses
a 1950s tractor and a mechanical muck spreader
a device that opens and closes the glasshouse windows
(minus four degrees, plus four degrees)
a caravan, truck used as storage
    volunteers:
    one has twin boys
    another has dreadlocks
    that one takes his kayak down the Ouse
four hundred boxes
leeks, potatoes, tomatoes, green leaves, imported fruit
invention, experiment, a mistake
shake the tomato plant, break off the shoots
say this one needs, that one needs
strong, bushy or lean, tall or squat, elegant
they need pampering
no blight here, no insects
hands wet with green oil, snakeskin
office, toilet, shed, bucket
planting leeks (sound of sheep, cows, birds, a mother)
make a hole with the spade handle or fork
deep enough
she could plant seven to his two
six rows, the length of that glasshouse

Homage

after Sylvia Plath's 'Yadwigha, on a Red Couch, Among Lilies'
A sestina for the Douanier

The word *homage* comes from the French word
for man, *homme* (a douanier on a red velvet couch
before a mille-fleurs tapestry perhaps) and describes
an act of feudal allegiance, fealty to one's lord
in honour of vassalage itself, with a ceremony where
the junior fellow goes bare-headed and weaponless
in a wilderness of heart-shaped leaves as a sign
of his submission to the will of his *seigneur*,
kneeling, red against green, the younger man
clasping his hands before him, body whiter
than a frill of lilies, and stretching out those hands
for the lord to take them in his in what is called
a 'handgang', a touching, to ensure the hierarchy,
the men now bonded like two birds of paradise;
and this gesture, this sacred, luminous touching,
is enacted still in the ceremony for conferring degrees
at Cambridge (where, as we know, she studied).
But how can we pay our debt and respects
in a modern way, how offer a Thesaurus of service
(tribute, loyalty, troth, fidelity, esteem, worship,
admiration, devotion, adulation, reverence, awe
or duty) without deference? Sometimes I cry out,
scored by her precision and wit, by her power
to eviscerate, to bleed us right there on the red couch,
surrounded by catalpa leaves, while she glows—
such red— under that vast and uncaged moon.

7th June

The cuckoo's call is continuous, almost
mechanical, a toneless echoing cu-cuh—

Above the continuity is the patterning
of the twitters, frills, whistles, chirps

cheeps, and other birds scissoring the air
snipping the air, using the air to warble

trill and mimic each other. And above that
a constant rattle of crickets, a circular

sound, or not entirely constant (imagine
the abdomens contracting, releasing)

and somewhere, bees are a humming fizz.
A cacophony: everything together holds

the air. And all the time, the cuckoo
not quite cu-cuh, cu-cuh, perhaps cu-huh.

Situation of secrecy

for *secrecy* you must hiss
smile, form a square
to make a 'cr'
in the mouth's roof
and hiss again
for the final 'cy'

say the truth—
make a groove for it
make a 'tr' behind the teeth
with air, note how the tongue
arrives late, its tip—
and 'th' is a light whistle

*

I will never write the live words

and the secret swims
between us
like an illness

*

the thing that happened
is the secret

the secret replaces the thing
that happened

*

secret is a child's word

what category of thing
is confession?

Interrupting the dreams of brick-makers

The first stage in the process, in the early autumn,
is to free the earth of stones, exposing it in small heaps
to coarse winter. By the time of the spring's rising,
the earth is ready to be kneaded or tempered.

Before it is burned, dry the brick out of the line of wind
or sun, letting the moisture be carried off slowly,
uniformly, from the surface. Apply a moderate fire
under the arches of the kiln for a day, a night.

Raise and lower the heat alternately until the burning
is complete. Clunch lime is good for waterworks,
harder than common chalk, with a low degree
of stony hardness, inclining to the colour of yellow ash.

I fly above myself as I think of her

I was at the hospital with her, my darling girl
(a headache starts above my blind right eye)

but I find today's self heals last month's self
and courts new images of whitening hillsides

whilst my plump plush family, even the dogs,
sit at a sumptuous table. I lie alongside them

on a narrow bed. I can be there or not there,
float up into a startling blue (which I allow

right inside for its grace) but now a madness
sucks away the back of my head, thick hands

place a milkmaid's yoke on my collar-bones
and she is cased in hard plastic, a young tree.

Soon, or later, we must let her go, let her go.

Foundry

The flame is lime
      lift the crucible   skim the slag
            it is love   it is love's failures
      the ones with the copper hair
who spit from their molten lips
      it is dry   dryer than anything he has known

A calibrated scratching—
      someone dressing in that corner
            smoothing down their clothes—
matter tapped   patted into form

He edges towards the centre
      speaks through roasted grain
            they need him
      him   he's deadly with that hammer
yet tenderly he shakes the small bag of lime powder

He is a friend of Hephaestus   he shines by day
      by vertical   by horizontal
            metal spits
the wound is made   and unmade
      it is a morality tale
            it is dryer than he has ever known

This is the hinterland between concentration and habit
      focus and dream
            it is barely knowledge   rather a knowing
      a move towards risk
            towards perfection

She gave him the wild ancient forest of Anderida
      exempt from tythe
because it owed nothing to man's labour.

I just wanted him to say sorry

On the first page, a black and white photograph
of Arthur Miller and his wife (not that one),
Inge Morath, in 1975—they're both laughing.

Next is a postcard of Botticelli's *Chart of Hell*
drawn on sheep's parchment with a metal stylus
using two types of ink, gold and isinglass jelly.

Mary Cassatt's 'The Sisters' lean sweetly out
from the next page, yet when a cloud passes over
the sun, I notice how very troubled they look.

Then there's Alan's true story: a girl on a bicycle
with her silver-gold hair flying out each side:
he felt her cycling right through his heart.

Opposite, on a small square of cardboard, the words
*'You can be happy if you can forgive. You must
always forgive.'* I know she is right, but I continue

to resist—until I encounter the next two postcards:
'No Woman, No Cry' by Chris Offili, the necklace
of jewel-blue tears released from one blue eyelid

and Käthe Kollwitz' charcoal drawing of the high
dark cheekbones of 'Prisoners listening to music'.

The offer

Some birds lay their eggs
on a rocky ledge
without any nest at all.
The guillemot, for example,
whose eggs (grey and black
with light grey patches)
roll in a circle,
shaped so they never fall.
Marsh-nesting birds tie
and close-weave,
and shearwaters use rabbit burrows.

She asked me—
her bantam chicks had died,
two chicks, one day old—
she asked me
if I would like to have them:
she could post them to me in a padded bag.
She asked me
if I would like to have her dead bantam chicks;
one day old when they died.
They had shrivelled a bit, she said,
the bantam chicks —

Swallows build tight
with mud and dried grasses,
lay a bed of small white feathers;
the coal tit gathers rabbit fur;
and the nightingale
creates a papery, fine-wafery
skeletal leaf-bowl: a loose,
leaky, reckless structure.

Swans in a field

two loop-necked birds
a strip of green
between them

nestled but alert
beaks reaching

I see them through glass
silent feathers

not far
from the stream

they arise from chaos
as traces of light

as movement
in the quiet green

small in the wide green

I am dazzled

I inhabit their emptiness

Participant observation

'*Early one morning, in the middle of the Brazilian jungle,*
I decided to take a swim
Looking to the right, I could see a room given over to camp beds
(bright green
in a beautiful waterfall. Afterward I sat on the edge of the rocks
to dry in the morning sun—
with pink sheets) in which people lay, eyes open, and some were
asleep without a bed.
and out of nowhere, a very clear thought struck me:
[…] that the gallery
Soon I was sitting my exam, sorting grains of rice from beans and
counting them.
should be completely empty. That the public would come in and
I would take them gently by the hand and bring them to a wall
I found I could persevere, for concentration itself, no one cared.
There were 297.
[…], just to look at the blank space in front of them.
To the left, on a low platform, a woman leaned on two crutches
as if without pain.
[…] The show would have no rules, no formula—just the artist,
the audience, and a few simple props in the empty white space.
Others were seated facing out, yet to be taken.
That the public become the performing body instead of me.
Someone came towards me, lowered her face a little.
[…The] visitors would go through various exercises:
just looking at the wall,
I found the thick silence.
counting grains, doing a slow-motion walk, lying on a cot
with eyes closed,
She said I could stay for as long as I wanted.
standing on a platform.' *
For as long as I wanted.

Inland

the gulls follow the ship
the men
the grief
the gulls follow
love follows
men grieve
the waiting is over
the ship is polished
a vision is coming
the new is following
the men follow the new
like gulls overhead
the men are overhead
the ship is overhead
follow the gulls
inland
the grief is inland
the grief is speaking
speak
speak
follow the words
words follow the men
the men in white
gulls in white
inland
an island of grief
a race
the gulls race overhead
in white grief
the men's white grief
follow the white
inland
white land
the men's white land
grief to the gulls
the white gulls
held in fear
heartbeat not my own
fear of grief

loss
fear of having another's heartbeat
on the white island
grief and fear on the white island
with the gulls
too much whiteness
and only the heart
which is inland
my heart is inland
the grief
is the hearts
of the men and the gulls
heartbeat borrowed
or lost
and the men field the white grief
which follows the ship
as love
and all on the white island
give them time on the inland island
where their hearts are white
bearing grief
and the gulls calling
in the white inland of the ship
and the men's white hearts
in the ship
on deck
in the loom
all inlaid
inland
all white
inlaid hearts
white grief
gulls and men
follow the white island of the heart
all inlaid in the heart
grief in the heart
in white
I find white in the heart
inlaid

Moss and me

There seems no surface
        only surface and depth at once

(the fronds yield, sway
        to the touch)

and when I look through
        the magnifying lens

I merely fall between the fronds
        towards Earth's core.

Korean diary

The building is plain, no insignia, three rough steps
up to the door. We encounter shoes, neatly in pairs

or abandoned, step further in, survey the low table.
We kneel, awkward, slip a thin cushion beneath us,

slide our legs under the wood. Our backs curve,
anticipate. The owner, cook, waitress is one woman:

she takes her time, serves us with a quiet neutrality.
First, a square of wet cloth for our hands, afterwards

kimchi, black beans in a sweet sauce, sesame leaves,
marinated radish, a long hot fish in a small bowl,

its head and tail intact; *bibimbap:* miso soup, bright
vegetables mixed with rice and chilli paste. We study

the form: with our metal chopsticks, we pincer leaves
and beans and rice, lower our eyes at our mistakes.

seeing in air

I

night reddening broad over red desert
over the scrag bush   pit pick of the fire
song of wild donkeys pulling up the air
dull-rub the flour and water   stretch
and drop   new sticks ticking on the heat
bury the damper under hot sand

brush sand off the damper and eat
while he speaks and speaks the land
—lay the dead emu over your heart
rub smoke in your face   your hair
so country can know you—

we're down in the swag   close to peace

II

the effort is to approach   reach
to apprehend the thirty portraits
holographic   three times life-size
alive in the unfinished air between us

your black hair is combed over your eyes
over your mouth

your face is patterned with the bars
of a bird cage

you are turned so we can testify
to your scars

your eyes follow me

from the test site at Maralinga
from the asbestos mine at Baryulgil
from the Hanging Tree

so many ill or burnt or wounded
so many

and no old words for this

Scatter my bright feathered heart

I made a bed to live or die in—
dark red buttons, gauze, a pillow
drawn from gentle rope.

The effort was to bear up, hold away
the weight, a cruel weight.
I cried at the pushing—

but I'm sailing now, breath is my sail—
the sun rolls over me
and air enters the body by quiet means.

Now, tears fold in, only tears, no one
to catch. There, have my heart—
it beats with or without me.

Bird of paradise flower

Strelizia reginae

The slender double-gold-collared sunbird
—a small passerine with a long arc'd bill—
leaves its purse-shaped lace-webbed nest
hung from a thin branch and darts down
for the nectar of a crane lily bird of paradise
flower, balances its seven grams on the petal-
leaf spathe and let-looses all the powdery
pollen, dusting its amethyst-orange breast
and feet, and flash-flies in the fireheart-heat
of the Western Cape to the next set of yellow-
red and bright blue tongues in horizontal
inflorescences - the envy of Charlotte, George
the Third's botanist wife from Mecklenburg-
Strelitz, an English queen of African descent.

The Colour of the Rhône at Verbois

I

I saw a river thick as butter churning,
  silent, layered strata, passing as if filmed—
    and my heart rushed towards the water, its milkiness—
I would hold it in my arms
  like a roll of silk, petrol blue and limestone grey—
    wide and fast, so fast, so wide
I could not draw myself away.
  I would wade in, be swept along like wood, pounded on the bank
    where I would linger, choking
until caught again by a muscled surge, and overwhelmed.
  I wanted this—silencing.
    I belonged to the river, to the Rhône at Verbois,
to its colour, force, its unconcerned flowing—bareback—
  towards the sea.
    And so I crept out along a branch,
lay down with one arm stretched
  above the water—felt the spray, the speed.
Suspended there I moaned and laughed in turn,
  listened to a wordless aching.

II

I walked and walked on rocks and narrow trails
   up and up towards the source.
     Rhythm of the hips—eight hours ascending—
past barns and timbered chalets—walked as if to discover the earth,
   walked, my hips, legs, feeling my bones—
     the straightness of my thigh bones,
my muscles—my feet landing square and square
   following the trail, narrow—one foot
     at a time climbing, towards the eyes of the silver cows,
amid bright blue gentians and the cries of marmots.
   Walking, each leg, the long bone working,
     rising into the sun, my pack dragging—
the feeling of ascent, the feeling of journey—
   each step taken a prayer, a promise—
     and this for no one.
Hips slowing—
   an eagle in the blue air—
     lichen giving the stones a pale green hue.

III

I'm here—seven or eight thousand feet up
  my fingers are numb—
   my lips are fizzing—
my lips are singed—and the Rhône Glacier
  sweeps down—
   the frozen water spills down over the moraines
its force pressing a gap in the rock,
  water expanding,
   layer upon layer of crystals and air pockets,
snowflakes trapped, longing—
  and long strips of old water loop down
   over sheer striated rocks—
a mad sweep of ice brushed down the mountain
  like maiden's hair, combed and falling,
   and the surprise
is the ice in bubbled chambers,
  tiny rivulets running here and there,
   swells and fans,
and all the time the smooth rocks beneath—
  high up on the Furkapass:
   the magnificent Rhonegletscher.

IV

I took the colour of the Rhône
  up the mountains,
    as if pushed upwards
by the weight, the surface of the water,
  by the velocity
    of the water,
as if the source were in the air—
  as if the source were uncontained
    by the outline of the river.
The lines of the river,
  lines stretched and waving
    course like a flaw or chasm
right through me,
  a terrible, un-swimmable liquid chasm,
    that blue un-navigable milkiness
saying to me, *lay down here,*
  my darling, in this fine swim
    lay down here
and every moment from here—each step,
  as the water pulls my face into soft distortion,
    each step towards the other side—
every moment is a small drowning.

Montana: 15th September

Third day in Small Town, Montana:
      one flat road through Ponderosa pines
cabins, trailers, long-beard bikers
      hotel, motel, casino
Make America Great Again Trump Fundraiser tonight
      two grizzly bears stuffed and mounted.

Yesterday, at dusk, I disturbed
      a Great Blue Heron
      drawing reluctantly from the creek
      an awkward rise, legs unfolding,
      its grace yet present in the sleek neck
      and slow effort
and I supposed, in wild nature, there could be no hurrying
      no mistakes, no greed or unkindness
      no taking for taking's sake
      no covenant-decreed sacrifice of others.

Then this afternoon I bought a potato-masher
      at the Variety Store,
      the shopkeeper's mother
was from Leeds, England, she said
      and there are too many I-ranians
      coming and taking our jobs
      and the President
      is letting them live right next door
      bringing in their bombs
      and they hate us, right
      so they can go right back home
      and leave the jobs for Americans
      for us Seniors, just trying to pay our taxes.

And to my right and to my left
      men ate wild Mallard
each an entire duck blooding their plates.

Now this evening, the creek below the pines
      is silver-pink
      shimmering toward the dark
and I think of the river running through us
      quietly asking its questions,
      low, beneath thought.

Untitled

less a sip than a gulp
stomach, ears
words at the bottom of the glass
uncertain
listen (remember, I didn't want this)
every time
tragic
every time—
they said, it happens
                (which is not reassurance)
they said
you know, excerpts, extracts
all the time now
huh
simplicity, somehow (when)
actually, I don't listen

Encounter

At once she showed us an image of the ashes of her friend —
a strongly-lit swirl against black, like a galaxy of stars
and so tactile that I stroked the image with my fingers.

She said that to arrange and photograph the ashes
was to take the dead's life forward, and presented a picture
of her own father inside the crematorium chamber,

his skull intact, the bones still laid down in human shape.
We saw, too, her reassembly of a museum's collection
of white, albino and transparent objects in tall vitrines:

a taxidermied swan, rabbits, fish and a pair of Victorian
silk button boots alongside two fur and diamond shoes
of her own. She used the word 'lucette'. Then we sat

at a long table where she explained the idea of *punctum*:
coming to a photograph with emotion first, under the radar
of learning or expectation—which did or did not prepare us

for a photo-work commissioned by the parents of an infant
who had died: the baby's ashes in a clear packet placed
above an old set of weighing scales, back-lit, and below,

pieces of bone in descending order of size, left to right,
measured against a brass ruler. Volume and length.
I thought of the John Berger story where a young man

falls into a furnace and disappears; his lover imagines him
forever in particles of the factory's dust—but here,
the beloved's remains were declared, illuminated, swept

into a ridge or scar. Afterwards, in grey light, we touched
the iron structure of a bassinet, remnant of an exhibition
of one hundred and forty antique rocking cradles displayed
in formal rows. Transformation through repetition, she said.

Afternoon out

I think nothing here, lying on the stones, listening to the water's twillup on my left and its huhhuhwilla on my right, and at one point, a singing starts up in my head, 'I stole my mother's...', and this is after sitting beneath the defences, wind rustling my flesh and walking back past a hedge of noisy birds and the secret message on the long fence: O WPCA/PNSY/LB33/ AK/ Y / 25 x 50 which I find I can translate, later, as:

dress sift wind of I / sails rise must love / I trade loss over fall/
I   you /ask love's more fail / fall is haven / this this all

In your presence

I heard a man say he could turn time into space
with twelve bottles of Turkish cologne,
an ivory shaving brush and evidence of waiting.

The day after, a lean man, a sinewy man, typed
my symptoms into his computer, it took
an hour, he could make no promises—

yet he opened the window a fraction, recommended
an app for staying alive, explained the word
'depersonalisation', let me charge my phone.

Later, our friends came by, radiantly, and we flew
over labyrinths, burst in and out of laughter
until darling served a luscious dish that rose and rose

in the charming heat and our oval faces lapped
at the sweetness. The next day, I stood upright
for a man who said 'do not deny your own violence,

do not interrupt the intelligence, yours or theirs, but
neither be sad or shy or punishing—instead, live
simply, cry out for the reasoning of kindness'.

After six days we were seeking answers, what I am,
you are, neither body nor mind, not two but one—
and I will not whisper 'consciousness' but drop it

from the lexicon, say uh-uh in its place, drift, sing
and dream freely, let new words blossom against
the night glass, trembling with spark-silver.

At the end, I showed you to the sun-draped bench,
we rested there together. I studied the slivers of scarlet
on your skin, saw at once—in time and space—

your flying heart, your echo heart,
the risks you'd taken, the lonely postmarks—
all that you had wrought and given.

Plaint

we couldn't reach you
couldn't interpret
the dry path you took
the light you cut
from the paper stems

we couldn't hold you
couldn't reach
behind the white wall
you cut

we saw you leaving
force stark petals
along our fingers

even then
especially then
your beauty
was not wrested from us

Yield

Cill Chainnigh, Kilkenny 2001

Airport: casual, walk straight down onto tarmac
inside, bowls of disinfectant for foot and mouth

Car: waiting at the Avis counter, Toyota Yaris
metallic green, Gaelic road signs, line of Garda

House: cul-de-sac, hibiscus on the windowsill
blue bed, silver fridge, a half-bottle of Jamieson's

Field: streams, ash, beech, wood white butterflies
ravens, the Wicklow Mountains, an unmade road

Quarry: limestone, dark pools, the gantry, crane
diamond drills, a spiral made from broken mortar

Story: a man you can't wear out, he talks and talks
gets lost at night, falls into space, clings to a tree

Books: all of Dervla Murphy, Philip Gourevitch's
genocide, Adrienne Rich's *What is Found There.*

Nomenclature II
or, Linnaeus takes (to) his bed

Carolus Linnaeus,
        also known as Carolus Linneus,
                remembered as Carl Linnaeus,
and ennobled as Carl von Linné,
        made a journey through Lapland in 1732
                with a portable bed made from a roll of moss
(carpet moss, *Mnium hornum*, presumably)

noting how birch leaves,
        gathered up at midsummer,
                were boiled with *Lycopodium Complanatum*
(Dwarf-Cypress moss)
        in the traditional dyeing of yarn
                for jackets and woollen leg-wraps
to a colour now known as
        New York Taxi Cab Yellow,

and wondering at babies asleep on *Spaghnum palustre*
        in smooth leather cradles
                lined with the hair of reindeer
herded by a dog and an agile maid-servant
        in heel-less boots,

also, counting hares and grey gnats
        and tuft-horned eagle owls,
                and eating coarse bread
        made from the inner bark of pine trees
        collected as the sap rises,

and, despite quite correctly distinguishing the male
        Bryum binum moss (stem and leaves
                of a blood-red hue, oblong,
pointed, and alternately imbricated)
        from the female
        (a long purple stalk,
pear-shaped pendulous head and very small veil)—
        foiling thereby the Hedwigian theory
                of the fructification of mosses—

46

Linnaeus Linneus von Linné
    later bowed to the eminence of Dillenius
        (family name formerly Dillen)
who died of apoplexy only six years after
    his natural history of mosses
        Historia muscorum appeared,

    so giving the ruby-red imbrication
    to the female and the tiny veil to the male
        and apparently with 'amiable deference'—

    (cushioned, no doubt, by his six-month long, two thousand-kilometer
    clockwise expedition round the misty Gulf of Bothnia
        with the moss bed,
finding silver mines *Gubbsilfver* and violet clay
    and country folk keeping sea-watch
        in the war with the Russians
and naming one hundred previously unidentified
    plant species—)
        but later, probably, with regret.

Oh,

we were out wide—
flying on the pull-high waves

rolling on the wet salt sting
lean and fro together, skirting

the red-grey rock, bird-white
rock, back and fro, wet wind

sing, face out strong, we were
trying to land, stop the wind

catch a single breath of still
sweet air, trying only to land.

When

He will make tea. I give him full instructions
on how to cure the problem of the chlorinated
water. I have a bath. I slip as I try to get out,
hurt my shin, foot, shoulder. I tell no one.
He will make toast: we will eat it with quince
and crab-apple jam and later, walk towards
the giant pendulum sequoia. We will gaze
at the river, say the word *glorious*, and I will
mention my conversation with P. in the hall
(he cannot remember, he said, all those years
ago: nothing), yet they say time is a cathedral,
and don't we have a duty to touch, try to touch
the things we knew? I will hear the sound
of muscled bird wings, a wasp on the glass.

Moss and me (2)

Moss is near,
it represents nearness.
I must bend or crouch close
for moss,
for what is spherical
or dry or yielding.
Moss is neither land
nor landscape.
It is (on) the ground
or it is a bark-swathe
or stump-drape,
speaking its green
to the high green
beech leaves.

The end of my imaginings

Images from *News from Nowhere* remain constant:
the river bank, tall houses, a ferry boat, a man,
a feeling of purity, and the colours are blue, stone,
light sand. Then those first moments: rough wood
of the long table, someone asking; diagonal of wet
striking my arm. Our ascent is slow, crowded.
A balcony is brightly lit, fern fronds hang down
from a fan or chandelier. Another table: blackness
on white linen, such bright greenness; the tang
of fish. Singly, men and women step forward,
the men substantial in their formal shoes. A light
is flickering. Perhaps someone is playing a piano.
My glass is empty. Women are approaching. I take
a tiny amount of the dark and know the meaning
of 'recoil'. The man beside me will not react
and soon I forget my experience, shape and scale
no longer reliable. There is only texture, there is
only contrast. Today, I recall my gratefulness—
I almost weep—for my piece of soft cloth.

Quiet series

I

it is a day of iridescent
       blue flies
       and realisations
the flies inside the room
       rain
the reckonings deep and absolute

II

we wait behind
       two shorn ewes and a lamb
       in the road
and talk about social housing
       and ideologues

III

August, the fennel is tall
       two globe artichokes
       still-tight red grapes
       we curse BT
       and unintended consequences
wet roses dead in full bloom

We unwrapped the vessels

Today we unwrapped the glass vessels,
laying down each one on the white cloth:
a hollow snake, three bowls, a horn
with opaque chambers, and two cylinders.
When we poured water in the horn we felt
the need to hold the horn close, rock it
a little, its curve becoming almost creaturely,
like the water in the large bowl when we
made it roll and gather until a bond formed,
keeping the water in a single sphere. And
when we found the indigo disc, its scale
suited to the space between human hands,
we saw how water spreads insistent, like
a staining. Another disc, large and clear,
we balanced on a glass plate to receive
a gentle water that pulled away to a drop,
suspended for a moment before it slipped
from the disc's perimeter. We noticed, too,
how quickly water forms a vortex, how
it creases and folds, casts a mercury bowl
if it's swirled in a tube with a concave base,
and also that water reflects the sky and trees
outside even when the glass doesn't.
Finally, just before the end, we unwrapped
the glass globe, and standing, held it
between us, close, at the level of our chests,
and a little lower, where the soul might rest.

Longing

we held our breath
waved a burnt red stick

called to a flock
of yellow birds

the sky was bitter

a bird fell down
another

from what was once
the canopy

Listening to moss

for Judith, i.m.

I take a blindfold, lie down and listen
to a half-globe of star-green star moss,
hear dense hairs ease up, and reflecting
leaf tips brace, catch narrow fronds sly
slowing the air, slow air lip a long leaf
and I just couldn't remember humanness
even though or especially because she died
and I wasn't there, nor she, all so very late
while the star-green star moss sips dew
in the breath-seed between air and rock
as if in death all were air and moss and fresh
floating love and death itself dissolved
until the powder-spores are lifted high,
full-free on breezy swirls and vortices.

Notes

In 'Participant observation' the italicised lines are from Marina Abramovich's memoir, *Walk through Walls*, where she imagines the show that became *512 Hours*, Serpentine Gallery.

'Encounter' describes the work of Canadian artist, Spring Hurlburt.

'Seeing in air II' is a response to *Unfinished Business: Stories about disability from remote, regional and urban Australian Aboriginal and Torres Strait Islander Communities*, State Library, Perth WA, 2016.